African-American Soldiers in the Revolutionary War

by Lucia Raatma

Content Adviser: Richard J. Bell, Ph.D.,
Assistant Professor, Department of History,
University of Maryland

Reading Adviser: Alexa L. Sandmann, Ed.D.,
Professor of Literacy, College and Graduate School of Education,
Kent State University

Compass Point Books ✦ Minneapolis, Minnesota

Compass Point Books
151 Good Counsel Drive
P.O. Box 669
Mankato, MN 56002-0669

This book was manufactured with paper containing
at least 10 percent post-consumer waste.

On the cover: *Desperate Valor,* painting of the Battle of Rhode Island, August 28, 1778,
by New England historical artist David R. Wagner

Photographs ©: David R. Wagner, cover, 22; Prints Old and Rare, back cover (far left); Library of Congress,
back cover, 6, 18, 24, 36; The Granger Collection, New York, 5, 9, 21, 23, 25, 30, 31, 32; North Wind
Picture Archives, 7, 19; Svetlana Zhurkin, 10; Rischgitz/Getty Images, 11; Bettmann/Corbis, 12; Library of
Congress/Printed Ephemera Collection, 13; U.S. Senate Collection/*General Marion Inviting a British Officer
to Share His Meal* by John Blake White, 16; Archive Photos/Getty Images, 17; Corbis, 27; From the Historical
Collection of the Stockbridge Library, 28; Jane Nocera, 29; Georgia Department of Archives and History,
33; Courtesy of The Historical Society Of Pennsylvania, detail of the portrait of James Forten, 34; National
Archives and Records Administration/Our Documents, 38; MPI/Getty Images, 40.

Editor: Jennifer VanVoorst
Page Production: Ashlee Suker
Photo Researcher: Svetlana Zhurkin
Cartographer: XNR Productions, Inc.
Library Consultant: Kathleen Baxter

Art Director: LuAnn Ascheman-Adams
Creative Director: Keith Griffin
Editorial Director: Nick Healy
Managing Editor: Catherine Neitge

Library of Congress Cataloging-in-Publication Data
Raatma, Lucia.
  African-American soldiers in the Revolutionary War / by Lucia Raatma.
    p. cm. — (We the people)
  Includes index.
  ISBN 978-0-7565-3848-4 (library binding)
1. United States—History—Revolution, 1775–1783—Participation, African American—
Juvenile literature. 2. African American soldiers—History—18th century—Juvenile literature.
I. Title. II. Series.
  E269.N3R33 2009
  973.3'408996073—dc22   2008007208

Visit Compass Point Books on the Internet at *www.compasspointbooks.com*
or e-mail your request to *custserv@compasspointbooks.com*

TABLE OF CONTENTS

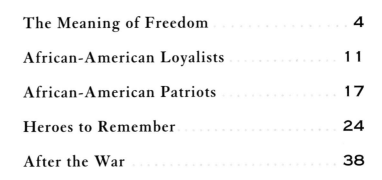

THE MEANING OF FREEDOM

The 1770s was an exciting period in the history of what is now the United States of America. Many people who lived in the 13 British-ruled American colonies began to long for freedom. They disliked being controlled by the British government, especially since they had no voice or representation in that government. These people, known as patriots, wished to form their own nation—a nation that provided freedom and liberty for everyone.

However, there was a noticeable irony in the colonists' plans. As they worked for their own freedom, they continued to deny it to the slaves they owned. Throughout the colonies, enslaved Africans worked long hours with no pay. They had no freedom to live where they wanted or choose how to make a living. Men, women, and children were bought and sold like livestock, and their families were often broken up during these sales.

Few patriots concerned themselves with this irony.

4

An 18th-century English tobacco label showed a plantation owner relaxing as enslaved Africans labored in the field.

Many of them, especially those in the South, became wealthy at the expense of the slaves they used in their fields and on their plantations. The rights of these black slaves seemed not to be as important as the rights of white men. While some leaders opposed slavery, others took part in the practice. George Washington and Thomas Jefferson, who would both become U.S. presidents, owned dozens of enslaved people who worked on their plantations.

President George Washington owned slaves to work the fields at his plantation, Mount Vernon.

The first enslaved Africans had arrived in the Virginia Colony in 1619. This original group was made up of about 20 people who had been captured in Africa and then transported to Jamestown by way of the Caribbean. But that number quickly grew. By 1775, when the Revolutionary War was about to begin, there were 500,000 slaves in the colonies. At this time, there was also a much

Africans were captured and sold into slavery—often by black slave traders who worked with white Europeans and Americans.

7

smaller number of free blacks. Free blacks were often of mixed-race backgrounds or were people who could not work as slaves, either because of age or physical injury.

Many enslaved people refused to accept slavery and ran away from their owners. Those who were caught were brutally punished. Some enslaved Africans tried to win their freedom in courts of law. After all, slavery was not legal in Great Britain. Why should it be legal in British colonies? A few enslaved people were successful in these efforts, but taking their owners to court was a long process. It was also difficult, since most slaves could not read or write.

In April 1773, a group of slaves petitioned the Massachusetts state legislature for their freedom. This group included Peter Bestes, Felix Holbrook, and Sambo Freeman. Part of their argument was that their slave status denied them basic rights. The petition read, in part: "We have no property! We have no wives! We have no children! No city! No country!" Their petition was largely ignored,

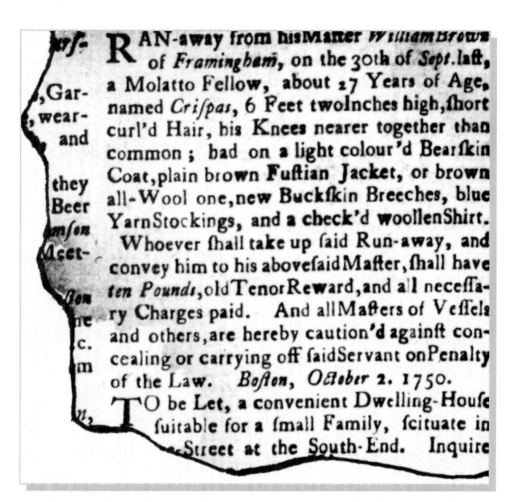

RAN-away from his Maſter *William Brown* of *Framingham*, on the 30th of *Sept.* laſt, a Molatto Fellow, about 27 Years of Age, named *Criſpas*, 6 Feet two Inches high, ſhort curl'd Hair, his Knees nearer together than common ; had on a light colour'd Bearſkin Coat, plain brown Fuſtian Jacket, or brown all-Wool one, new Buckſkin Breeches, blue Yarn Stockings, and a check'd woollen Shirt. Whoever ſhall take up ſaid Run-away, and convey him to his aboveſaid Maſter, ſhall have *ten Pounds*, old Tenor Reward, and all neceſſary Charges paid. And all Maſters of Veſſels and others, are hereby caution'd againſt concealing or carrying off ſaid Servant on Penalty of the Law. *Boſton*, *October* 2. 1750.

TO be Let, a convenient Dwelling-Houſe ſuitable for a ſmall Family, ſcituate in Street at the South-End. Inquire

A notice in the Boston Gazette *offered a reward for escaped slave Crispus Attucks, who would later die in the Boston Massacre.*

so they resubmitted it in May 1774. Again, no legal action was taken.

The Declaration of Independence, which was written and signed during the American Revolution, began with

The Declaration of Independence outlined the beliefs of the Founding Fathers.

this statement: "We hold these truths to be self-evident, that all men are created equal, that they are endowed by their Creator with certain unalienable Rights, that among these are Life, Liberty and the pursuit of Happiness." But the Founding Fathers did not feel that these unalienable rights—which are fundamental human rights—applied to African-Americans as well.

10

AFRICAN-AMERICAN LOYALISTS

It is difficult to imagine the hardships that enslaved
Africans faced. They were taken from their homes, put on
ships, and transported to the colonies. They were denied
all personal freedom. Slaves sometimes talked about

*The trip from Africa to North America gave enslaved people a sense of the hardship
that was to come.*

rebelling against their owners. Some mistakenly believed a rumor that the British would let any slave who put his owner to death have control of his owner's land. The slaves held secret meetings and tried to come up with plans to overpower their owners.

There were actually very few large-scale slave revolts, but slave owners remained in fear of the possibility. Controls on the slaves were tightened. Many slaveholders

Slave owners punished enslaved people who rebelled against their circumstances.

patrolled country roads late at night. Any slaves caught meeting in groups or out after dark were beaten or sometimes killed.

The British government knew that the slaves were angry, so they encouraged them to run away and join the British forces. The slaves had the idea that the British would treat them better than their owners had. This was not necessarily the case.

In November 1775, Lord Dunmore, the British governor of the Virginia Colony, issued a proclamation that freed the slaves and invited them to join the British army. This act led to thousands of slaves running away from their masters and

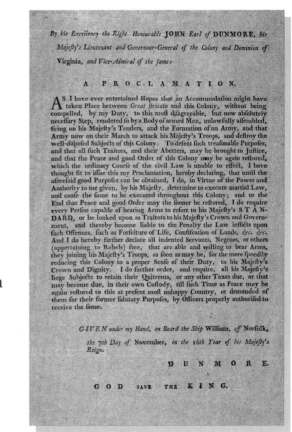

Lord Dunmore's 1775 proclamation

fleeing to British ships.

The following month, about 300 of these men formed Lord Dunmore's Ethiopian Regiment. They wore uniforms with the words "Liberty to Slaves." This group fought at the Battle of Great Bridge, and Dunmore felt the regiment held tremendous promise. But a wave of smallpox hit the regiment, and many of the men died from the disease. Dunmore abandoned the regiment on an island.

Although Dunmore's group was hard hit, many more slaves continued to run away. It is estimated that nearly 100,000 enslaved people joined the loyalist cause during the American Revolution. While some became soldiers, others chose to leave the colonies. These refugees escaped to British territories in Canada and the Caribbean, as well as to the African nation of Sierra Leone.

In 1961, historian Benjamin Quarles published a book called *The Negro in the American Revolution.* This was one of the first serious discussions of the role of African-Americans in the war. In the preface to the book,

African-American soldiers on both sides of the conflict fought in many battles of the Revolutionary War.

he explained how they decided which side to favor: "The Negro's role in the Revolution can best be understood by realizing that his major loyalty was not to a place nor to

An African-American soldier served as cook at a meeting between a patriot and British officer.

a people but to a principle. Insofar as he had freedom of choice, he was likely to join the side that made him the quickest and best offer in terms of those 'unalienable rights' of which Mr. Jefferson has spoken."

AFRICAN-AMERICAN PATRIOTS

In the years leading up to the Revolutionary War, many colonists dared to protest British practices. These patriots spoke out against unfair taxes and other laws. British soldiers occupied the city of Boston, Massachusetts, to maintain control there.

One man who protested the British presence was Crispus Attucks. This former slave was a free man who worked on whaling ships. On March 5, 1770, he took part in a demonstration in Boston that turned violent. The crowd began throwing ice, snowballs, and rocks at the soldiers. In the chaos and confusion, the soldiers fired their weapons, and Attucks was among the five people who were

Crispus Attucks

17

killed. This incident became known as the Boston Massacre, and news of it inspired many patriots to stand up to the British. Although the actual conflict would not begin for another five years, Attucks is considered to be one of the first Americans to die in the Revolutionary War.

The first battles of the Revolutionary War took place in April 1775 in the Massachusetts towns of Lexington and Concord. British soldiers were marching toward these towns to take control of weapons and ammunition that patriots were storing there. Paul Revere rode ahead, warning

A Boston newspaper memorialized four of the victims of the Boston Massacre.

the townspeople of the British advance. Soldiers known as Minutemen, because they could be ready for battle in a minute, prepared to face the British troops. Among the Minutemen were African-Americans Peter Salem of Framingham, Cato Stedman and Cuff Whitemore of

Minutemen were called to battle when the British marched on Lexington, Massachusetts.

Cambridge, Samuel Craft of Newton, and Isaiah Bayoman of Stoneham.

However, only a month after those battles, the Massachusetts legislature stated that slaves were prohibited from serving in the patriot army. Many leaders worried about how slaveholders would react if their slaves were taken away from them to join the army. Some leaders feared what would happen if slaves were given weapons. Could they be trusted to fight the British? Or would they turn on the people who had enslaved them?

By the end of 1775, George Washington, commander of the Continental Army, began allowing free blacks into his army of patriots. Enslaved blacks were still prohibited. As the war progressed, however, some slaves entered the war in a different way. When white slaveholders were called to serve in the armed forces, they sometimes offered up their slaves as substitutes. This practice began in 1777 when New Jersey's Militia Act allowed slaveholders to send slaves to fight in their place.

The Continental Navy was in desperate need of men, so recruitment was open to African-Americans throughout the war. Though captains were white, many African-Americans proudly served on naval ships.

Throughout the Revolution, some armies were integrated, allowing for blacks and whites to fight together.

A 1781 illustration of Revolutionary War soldiers featured a black light infantryman.

In Connecticut, Massachusetts, and Rhode Island, though, there were all-black units. The Rhode Island regiment fought a battle on Aquidneck Island in August 1778. For four hours, these men held off the British army and allowed a patriot army to escape. Today a monument that commemorates their courage stands in Portsmouth, Rhode Island.

Artist David R. Wagner's painting Desperate Valor *depicts the Rhode Island regiment fighting in the battle of Rhode Island in August 1778.*

Thousands of African-Americans served in the patriot army.

Life for members of patriot armies was very difficult. These soldiers were mostly untrained. The skills they really had were those of carpenters, farmers, shopkeepers, and fishermen. The army was not as organized as that of the British, so clothing, food, and medicine were in short supply. On a daily basis, most patriot soldiers were tired, dirty, and hungry.

Many African-American soldiers faced British troops in combat. They also dug trenches, built bridges, and cleared swamps for General Washington's troops.

By 1779, the number of troops in the Continental Army was very low. Washington opened up enlistment to all African-Americans, free or slave. However, treatment of blacks was far from fair, and none ever rose above the rank of private.

23

HEROES TO REMEMBER

In the almost 250 years since the American Revolution, many names have become well-known. Paul Revere made the famous ride from Boston to alert the Minutemen. Thomas Jefferson wrote the first draft of the Declaration of Independence. George Washington led patriot troops to ultimate victory. However, few people know the African-American soldiers who made their mark.

One of these soldiers was William Lee, who spent many days by George Washington's side. In fact, some say that Lee was Washington's closest companion during the war. It is said that this friendship inspired Washington

General Washington was painted with an African-American servant.

to believe that slavery should be outlawed, although Washington did nothing to bring this to pass. He made arrangements to free Lee in his will, providing him with food, clothing, and $30 a year (a rather large sum at the time) for the rest of his life.

Prince Whipple was a soldier who many believe is featured in the famous painting *Washington Crossing the Delaware.* Part of a wealthy family in Africa, Whipple

In Emanuel Leutze's painting Washington Crossing the Delaware, *many believe the black soldier (face hidden) in the bow of the boat to be Prince Whipple.*

came to the American colonies at the age of 10 to get an education. The captain of his ship sold him into slavery instead. Prince was bought by William Whipple of New Hampshire and accompanied him during the war, serving in the Battle of Saratoga, New York, in 1777, and the Battle of Rhode Island in 1778. After the war, he and about 20 other enslaved people petitioned the New Hampshire legislature for their freedom. They claimed that they had been born free in Africa and that, according to the Declaration of Independence, freedom is a right of all and cannot be taken away by force. He was freed soon after, in 1784.

Private Peter Salem fought in the battles of Lexington and Concord, but he made history at the Battle of Bunker Hill in June 1775. As the British troops advanced, the patriots were reportedly ordered, "Don't fire till you see the whites of their eyes!" Salem obeyed orders and waited as the British got closer. In the lead, British Major Pitcairn called, "The day is ours!" Salem fired and killed him. Salem

Peter Salem became a hero after shooting Major Pitcairn in the Battle of Bunker Hill.

was hailed as a hero and went on to fight in the 1777 Battle of Saratoga and others.

In 1777, an 18-year-old free black named Agrippa Hull enlisted in the Massachusetts brigade. He served for more than six years, mostly under the command of General Thaddeus Kosciuszko, a Polish general who was helping the patriot cause. Hull survived battles in Saratoga and in Eutaw Springs, South Carolina. When the war was over, he

Agrippa Hull

settled in Stockbridge, Massachusetts. Today his portrait hangs in the Stockbridge library.

In the summer of 1777, Washington's Continental Army faced the British at the Battle of Brandywine. Edward Hector played a key role. Hector was an artilleryman, which meant he was in charge of weapons and ammunition. During a fearsome British advance, many patriots began to run, leaving their wagons, horses, guns, and ammunition. Hector realized that those items should not fall into the hands of the British. He was ordered to abandon his artillery wagon, but he shouted, "Never! I'll save my horses or die myself!" He did, in fact, save his horse-drawn wagon and all its supplies, allowing Washington to be ready for battle the next time. In 1834,

90 years old and nearing death, the legislature of Pennsylvania awarded him $40. This was the only payment he ever received for his brave service.

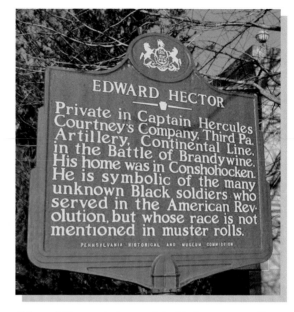

Edward Hector is honored in his hometown of Conshohocken, Pennsylvania.

In 1781, George Latchom showed his bravery in a battle in Virginia. Colonel John Cropper was leading a small group of militia against a group of British soldiers. By his side was Latchom, the slave of a neighbor. As the two men crossed some marshland, Cropper sank in the mud up to his waist. Latchom shot an approaching enemy soldier, then grabbed Cropper under the arms and pulled him free. After both men were safe, Cropper bought Latchom from his owner and gave him his freedom.

Salem Poor enlisted in Andover, Massachusetts, and fought in the Battle of Bunker Hill. During that battle, he

Several African-American soldiers earned renown in the Battle of Bunker Hill.

shot and killed Lieutenant Colonel James Abercrombie
of the British army. Fourteen fellow soldiers petitioned
Congress to reward him for his bravery on that day, but
there is no record that an award was ever granted. Poor also

fought in White Plains, New York, and endured the long, cold winter of 1777–1778 with General Washington and his troops at Valley Forge.

One of the most successful spies of the American Revolution was James Armistead. He spied on Benedict Arnold, who was an American traitor. He also managed to become part of the staff of British General Charles Cornwallis. He sent military information to the Marquis de Lafayette, a French soldier who served with the patriot army

A contemporary French engraving of James Armistead and the Marquis de Lafayette

31

during the war. This information helped the patriots win the Battle of Yorktown in 1781. After the war, Armistead became James Armistead Lafayette, taking the French hero's name as his own. He received a letter of commendation from Lafayette and was eventually granted his freedom.

James Armistead Lafayette

Born a slave in North Carolina, Austin Dabney joined the army when his owner sent him in his place. He fought in the Battle of Kettle Creek in Georgia and was shot in his thigh. Unable to walk for some time after the injury, he was cared for by a family named Harris. In gratitude, he worked for many years in the Harris household and helped send the oldest son to college. In

1819, Dabney was not allowed to take part in a lottery for land given to Revolutionary War veterans. Rightfully, the Georgia legislature later awarded him 112 acres (45 hectares) for his "bravery and fortitude." Initially many whites protested this award, saying that black veterans

Austin Dabney petitioned the state and was awarded his share of the land granted to veterans.

should not be treated like white ones. Eventually, however, Dabney won over his neighbors and became friends with some of the wealthy landowners.

James Forten was an amazing young man. At age 15, this free black served on the *Royal Louis,* a patriot ship that fought British ships. At one point, he was taken prisoner by the British. The captain's son became friendly with Forten and offered him the opportunity to escape to a comfortable life in England. But Forten refused to betray his country. He remained prisoner with 1,000 others on the *Jersey,* which was anchored near New York. Later, he had a chance to escape in a chest that was being moved off the ship, but he gave up that spot to allow a younger

James Forten

34

boy to escape. Several months later, Forten was freed in an exchange between the Americans and the British. He walked home to Philadelphia and went on to be a leader in the abolition movement, which worked to outlaw slavery.

One woman who played a key role in this era in American history was Phillis Wheatley. She may not have worn a soldier's uniform, but she fought her own battle with words. As an 8-year-old girl, she was taken from her home in Africa and sold as a slave in Massachusetts. The Wheatley family of Boston saw that she was sickly, and they wanted to help her. Their own daughter, Mary, was also not healthy.

Once in the Wheatley household, Phillis learned to read and write, and she spent many hours with Mary. By age 12, she began writing poetry. Many of her poems talked about religion and criticized the practice of slavery. In 1773, Mary's brother, Nathaniel, took Phillis to London with him. While they were there, a British publisher agreed to publish her book of poems, which had been rejected by American printers. The book was called *Poems on Various Subjects, Religious and Moral.* She continued to write poetry and gained recognition throughout the colonies and the world. She even wrote about and met George Washington. Today there is a monument in Boston in her honor.

The title page of Phillis Wheatley's book featured a portrait of the author.

Throughout the American Revolution, thousands of African-Americans did their part for the patriot cause. But we will never know who they were because most regiments did not take the time to record the names of African-American soldiers. The heroes—known and unknown—who helped make the United States independent proved that African-Americans had the skill and the courage to play key roles in the founding of the country. They may not have had the rights that white soldiers did, but they possessed bravery and loyalty that inspired others and perhaps planted the seeds to end slavery.

AFTER THE WAR

Records show that only a few African-American soldiers received military pensions after the war. Some of these soldiers were given their freedom, but they still remained citizens with few rights. And some of these soldiers who helped their nation gain freedom were forced to return to a life of slavery.

When the U.S. Constitution was written in 1787, the practice of slavery was protected. This was probably a way to make sure the

The Constitution of the United States of America

southern colonies would agree to the Constitution, but many people were angered by it. One was the Marquis de Lafayette, who later wrote, "I would never have drawn my sword in this cause of America could I have conceived that thereby I was founding a land of slavery."

In spite of their noble service during the American Revolution, African-Americans were quickly eliminated from military service. In 1792, Congress passed a law that restricted military duty to "free, able-bodied white male citizens." In 1798, when the Marine Corps was founded, "no Negro, mulatto [mixed-race person] or Indian" was allowed to enlist.

After the American Revolution, many northern states began to free slaves and outlaw slavery. But the southern states felt that slavery was a necessary part of their lifestyle, providing labor to plant and harvest the crops on their plantations. In 1863, President Abraham Lincoln signed the Emancipation Proclamation during the Civil War. The proclamation freed enslaved people in states that were rebelling against the Union. It also allowed the newly freed slaves to join the U.S. military. Nearly 200,000 African-Americans fought in the Civil War as soldiers in the Union Army or sailors in the Navy. Slavery was finally brought to an end in 1865 when the Union Army overran the last slave plantations.

African-American soldiers served in large numbers in the Civil War.

In 1855, Harriett Beecher Stowe, the author of the antislavery novel *Uncle Tom's Cabin,* wrote the introduction to *The Colored Patriots of the American Revolution,* by William Cooper Nell. In referring to those African-American soldiers who fought in the Revolutionary War, she explained, "It was not for their own land they fought, not even for a land which had adopted them, but for a land which had enslaved them, and whose laws, even in freedom, oftener oppressed than protected. Bravery, under such circumstances, has a peculiar beauty and merit."

GLOSSARY

abolition—immediate end of something, such as slavery

colonies—13 British territories that became the United States of America

commendation—formal praise

irony—result that is the opposite of what was intended

loyalists—colonists who remained loyal to the British government

patriots—American colonists who wanted their independence from Britain; people who love their country

pensions—payments of money given to people who have retired from their jobs

petitioned—signed a letter asking people in power to take action on a certain issue

private—soldier of the lowest rank

regiment—military group made up of about 1,000 soldiers

traitor—someone who aids the enemy and betrays his or her own country

DID YOU KNOW?

- After the Boston Massacre and the death of Crispus Attucks, Paul Revere made an engraving of the event. Thousands of copies were distributed throughout the colonies, which helped the patriot cause gain strength. It is one of the most famous engravings in U.S. history. However, in the engraving, Attucks is shown as being white.

- By 1777, white men who enlisted in the army were paid bonuses of $1,000. Black men were paid only $100.

- In 1779, about 550 black volunteers from the French-owned island of Haiti enlisted in the war and fought on the American side.

- In his will, Polish General Thaddeus Kosciuszko directed that a parcel of land he owned in Ohio be sold and the proceeds used to purchase and free slaves and provide for their education. After his death, the money from the sale of the land was used to found a school for African-Americans in Newark, New Jersey.

IMPORTANT DATES

Timeline

1770	Crispus Attucks dies during the Boston Massacre.
1775	In April, African-Americans are among the Minutemen who fight at Lexington and Concord, the first battles of the American Revolution; in May, Congress declares that slaves cannot fight in the army; in December, approximately 300 men join Lord Dunmore's Ethiopian Regiment.
1777	New Jersey allows slaveholders to offer up their slaves as their substitutes in the war.
1778	An all-black unit fights a battle at Aquidneck Island in Rhode Island.
1779	General Washington welcomes all African-Americans—free or slave— into the Continental Army.
1787	The U.S. Constitution protects the practice of slavery.
1792	Congress restricts military service to "free, able-bodied white male citizens."

IMPORTANT PEOPLE

JAMES ARMISTEAD LAFAYETTE (1748–1830)

One of the most successful spies of the Revolutionary War; the information he provided helped the patriots win the Battle of Yorktown in 1781; he became a farmer after the war

JAMES FORTEN (1766–1842)

Free black soldier who was taken prisoner by the British and twice refused offers of escape; he was eventually released and went on to be a successful businessman in Philadelphia; he made sails for ships, was an inventor, and was one of the early leaders of the abolition movement

PETER SALEM (1750–1816)

Soldier who killed British Major Pitcairn in the Battle of Bunker Hill; he also fought in the battles of Lexington and Concord, the Battle of Saratoga, and others; he worked as a weaver after the war

PRINCE WHIPPLE (1750–1796)

Soldier who served in the Battle of Saratoga in 1777 and the Battle of Rhode Island in 1778; a slave, he was owned by William Whipple, one of the signers of the Declaration of Independence; many believe he is the soldier featured in the famous painting Washington Crossing the Delaware

WANT TO KNOW MORE?

More Books to Read

Davis, Burke. *Black Heroes of the American Revolution.* Orlando, Fla.:
Odyssey Classics, 2007.

Haskins, Jim, ed. *Black Stars of Colonial and Revolutionary Times: African
Americans Who Lived Their Dreams.* New York: John Wiley, 2002.

Kallen, Stuart A. *Life During the American Revolution.* San Diego:
Lucent Books, 2002.

Rappaport, Doreen, and Joan Verniero. *Victory or Death!: Stories of the
American Revolution.* New York: HarperCollins, 2003.

On the Web

For more information on this topic, use FactHound.

1. Go to *www.facthound.com*

2. Type in this book ID: 0756538483

3. Click on the *Fetch It* button.

FactHound will find the best Web sites for you.

On the Road

American Independence Museum

One Governors Lane

Exeter, NH 03833

603/772-2622

Exhibits about the soldiers who served the patriot cause during the American Revolution

Bunker Hill Monument

Boston National Historical Park

Charlestown Navy Yard

Boston, MA 02129

617/242-5642

Monument commemorates the battle of the Revolutionary War in which African-American soldier Peter Salem killed Major Pitcairn

Look for more We the People books about this era:

The Articles of Confederation

The Battle of Bunker Hill

The Battle of Saratoga

The Battles of Lexington and Concord

The Bill of Rights

The Boston Massacre

The Boston Tea Party

The Declaration of Independence

The Electoral College

Great Women of the American Revolution

Inventions of the 1700s

The Minutemen

Monticello

Mount Vernon

Paul Revere's Ride

The Second Continental Congress

Shays' Rebellion

The Surrender of Cornwallis

The U.S. Constitution

Valley Forge

A complete list of We the People titles is available on our Web site:
www.compasspointbooks.com

INDEX

About the Author

Lucia Raatma is a freelance writer who has written books about history, safety, wildlife, and famous people. When she is not researching or writing, she enjoys going to movies, practicing yoga, and spending time with her husband and their two children. She lives in New York.